Gaslighting

*Break Free of Narcissistic and Manipulative Control
and Recover from Emotional Abuse for Good
(2022 Guide For Beginners)*

Contents

INTRODUCTION

CONSIDER THIS SCENARIO FOR A MOMENT.

Y ou've had a disagreement with a friend or partner about something. This "something" could be minor or large, but whatever the topic of conversation, the other person has made you feel, well, confused and twisted. Perhaps it even left you doubting yourself and feeling as though things weren't as they looked, even if you were certain they were. This is a type of exploitation known as gaslighting. This perplexity could manifest itself in a variety of ways. Perhaps that individual has made you feel emotional and exploited an insecurity you have, exacerbating how you feel while fully aware of what they are doing and how they make you feel. Perhaps you've been convinced that something happened, or you've felt a certain way when something deep down tells you that this isn't the truth. This has been a recurring problem in my life. I was fed up with my father, an abusive man who abused both my mother and me the same way. Similar things have happened to me in some friendships and love relationships. It's happened in the workplace and among grandparents, according to accounts I've heard. Allow me to give you a simple example.

Assume you're with someone and you arranged to have a date night on Friday. Friday night arrives, and you get dressed, and then they say, "Oh no, I said Saturday night." I'm quite busy tonight. You're a moron!" It's important to remember that this does not necessarily imply that your partner is gaslighting you in this circumstance. Maybe they did tell you the wrong day, or maybe you just misheard them and got the dates mixed up. That does happen on occasion. When this becomes a frequent occurrence, difficulties begin to surface.

I'm going to get to the point quickly. Control is exercised through gaslighting. You might wonder why someone would bother lying about something as insignificant as when their date night was or what their favourite takeaway is. But it all boils down to one simple concept.

CONTROL

Putting someone down and making them feel that they're either not paying attention to what's being said or that they're foolish or silly because they can't recall things correctly is a manner of putting someone down and gripping the back of their foot in a relationship. The person being gaslighted feels shame for not being good enough, which might lead them to try harder and harder, giving the person conducting the gaslighting even more power over the situation.

IS THIS STARTING TO SOUND FAMILIAR?

Whether you've heard about gaslighting before, been given this or a similar book, or have experienced these scenarios yourself, here is your first reminder that you don't have to live this way. Being manipulated by someone in your life, whether in a personal or professional relationship, is not acceptable, and you do not have to put up with it. But, for the time being, I'd like to slow things down and go back to the beginning. We'll go over everything you need to know about gaslighting in this book, including what it is, where it comes from, how to recognise it, how to prevent it, and, most crucially, how to get out of a gaslighting situation.

While we will first focus on gaslighting, including topics such as what it is, where it originates from, and warning signs, we will also go into toxic relationships of all kinds, how to detect them, how to deal with them, and offering tips on how to get out of them. These prompts will assist you in guiding your thoughts to recognise the type of abuse you are experiencing and what to look out for in your relationships. It then all comes together to provide you the attitude and information you need to deal with the abuse effectively, as well as advice for what to do next. Nonetheless, you'll see what I mean as you progress through the book, but just to make sure we're all on the same page, let's start at the beginning.

THE ORIGINS OF GASLIGHTING

Surprisingly, the phrase "gaslighting" has been around for a long time. The concept initially featured in the 1938 theatrical play Gas Light; a mystery thriller created by British dramatist Patrick Hamilton. There were further cinematic adaptations made in 1940 and 1944.

The screenplay's plot is straightforward. The main character in the play attempts to persuade his wife and others in his life that she is insane by modifying, manipulating, and controlling their home and the overall atmosphere in which they live. Of course, the wife is not mad, so when she wonders why things are somewhat off, he tries to convince her that she is mistaken, delusional, or has a bad memory. According to the title of the play, the most common way he accomplishes this is by gradually dimming their home's gaslights and then pretending nothing has changed. A more in-depth narrative follows the premise that he murdered a woman and is seeking for her lost valuables. Having his wife evaluated and admitted to a mental institution will enable him to search more easily and gain her power of attorney.

However, like the modern definition of the phrase, gaslighting is all about gaining control over someone in a manipulative and emotionally harmful manner. Consider how someone who has been subjected to these kinds of behaviours for several years will feel about themselves. Maybe, like me, you don't need to think too hard.

Since the play and films were released, psychologists and laypeople have used gaslighting to illustrate psychopathic behaviour. There is no doubting that acting in this manner is a harsh act of employing psychological efforts to confuse and call into question someone's reality or cognitive soundness. It is a severe form of psychological mistreatment in which the victim frequently questions whether the memories, feelings, or experiences they have experienced are authentic.

The individual who conducts this manipulative mental tactic, referred to throughout this book as the "gaslighter," can take advantage of the victim's fragile state of mind by presenting incorrect information in order to be seen favourably. The victim is then completely under the influence of the gaslighter, who forces them to believe whatever narrative they want them to believe. Gaslighting abuse impacts dozens, if not hundreds of thousands, of people around the world, and it is a subject that is extremely important to my heart. As a mother of two children, I have had firsthand knowledge of gaslighting. For nearly 10 years, I laboured in a poisonous relationship, an intimate relationship that I rationalised in my head over and over, no matter what happened. I was able to open my eyes one day and really see my relationship for what it was.

Guess who it is. It was my first marriage, and it was by far the worst experience I'd ever had. The assault was very psychological, as it frequently is, in order to instil doubts in my mind in order to fully brainwash me. I was steadfastly committed to the marriage, as one would be when married to the alleged love of one's life, but he was an outstanding liar. In retrospect, I should have known he was a compulsive liar from the start, but I always imagined that I would be the one to convert him into a better person, and I loved him, so I accepted him exactly as he was. It was my destiny to be with him, to love him, and to dedicate myself to him. Ah, the innocence of love, don't you think?

I'll go over my unique experiences with you in greater depth later, but let me start with this and see if it sounds familiar. My mistaken trust in my husband and our relationship prompted me to second-guess myself at every turn and on every detail. I frequently apologised to him for my "craziness." I had lost my self-esteem and sense of self. I was on the point of losing my mind since the settings I found myself in had such a large impact on my views, reality, and psyche.

However, as I was introduced to gaslighting and other forms of psychological abuse, I became informed and began to recognise what was going on in my relationship and how I wasn't being treated properly. I quickly recognised that I had been duped. I eventually decided it was time to leave the marriage, but it took a long time for me to regain some mental and emotional equilibrium.

Gaslighting is not a one-time or transient event; it persists indefinitely until the problem is illuminated. In fact, the more it happens, the worse the consequences get. It's similar to a snowball effect. The more it happens, the lower the victim's self-esteem and the more powerful the perpetrator gets. Concealment is a hallmark of this mental and emotional abuse, and it allows gaslighting to thrive.

CHAPTER ONE

WHAT EXACTLY IS GASLIGHTING?

GASLIGHTING

G aslighting affects everyone, and anyone can become a victim of this most insidious of psychological tricks. It is all about obtaining power over someone else by manipulating their thinking.

How we perceive and react to our surroundings impacts who we are, who we become, and how we see and react to the world around us. Perception is our "mind-made model of the world" (Fahkry, 2018). When someone changes that perception, they get the power to change our reality for their own selfish interests. Taking that power renders you, the victim, weak and unable to return to your true self. With this loss of authority comes uncertainty, a terrible sense of insecurity, and the loss of your freedom to live your life based on your own decisions. It is instinctive to gravitate toward a powerful character in your life–in this case, the narcissist or gaslighter who appears to be your rescuer. Despite the fact that they are the source of your instability and emotional anguish, you resort to the offender for assistance, playing right into their hands. Gaslighters use their victims' realities against them. They manipulate events, memory, emotions, and even how their victims react to their surroundings in order to gain an advantage and influence how the victim perceives their world. They take control of their victim's life, and the victim becomes reliant on the abuser for approval. Because there are no outward indicators of abuse, this is the most insidious form of emotional abuse. There will be no slurs or physical abuse, such as being beaten by your partner. Instead, the abuse emerges as a loss of authority and emotional retreat as the perpetrator of gaslighting takes control of your life and becomes your universe.

This is a phenomenon that is most commonly observed inside the confines of partnerships, yet the relationship does not have to be romantic. We have probably all been victims of gaslighting at some point in our lives, whether at work, among colleagues, at home with siblings, or in our social circles among friends. Most likely, you are unaware that you have been duped. And therein lays the risk. It is a sort of abuse that is tough to admit to suffering from since the abuser has co-opted our power to revolt. In a nutshell, gaslighting is harmful.

EXPLANATION OF GASLIGHTING

We all want to feel powerful. We prefer to believe that we are the best or that we are superior than others. It is an instinct that may have its origins in primordial times when cave-humans chose their mates based on thoughts of supremacy. Being the best necessitates discernment. Your worth is determined by how it compares to the worth of those around you. In your workplace, you may be able to confidently assert that you are a good worker (or indispensable to the company) based on how you compare to your peers.

That explanation, in my opinion, is perfectly valid. However, when you begin actively (or even subconsciously) undermining the other person, the judgement equation shifts in your favour, you have begun gaslighting. You are therefore stealing power from the other person in order to advance your cause or achieve your goals. The bizarre part is that the process of gaslighting has its own benefits, which, of course, encourages greater manipulation and reality distortion. The gaslighter will see that their efforts have given them a sense of authority because their victim has either lost power or comes to them for instruction, so stroking the gaslighter's ego (so to speak).

A gaslighter may approach you at work and say that you are making too many errors in a task (which you may not be making). They will not do so in an argumentative or suspicion-inspiring manner. Instead, they will appear to be your bosom pal who is only looking out for you. As a result, you will feel uneasy and will seek counsel and reassurance from this "friend," opening the door to additional deception. The payoff for the gaslighter is that they feel required by you and enjoy tugging your strings. They like the power that comes with watching your world slowly slide out of control. "You're both repulsed and hooked [to the gaslighter] at the same time," writes Stephanie Sarkis (Gillihan, 2018). You realise at some level that this person is not good for you and that they are controlling you to do things that are not in your best interests, but instead of fleeing, you are pulled to them. They win you over with charisma (presenting a personality type you like), certainty ("I am your buddy, and all I want for you is the best"), and guilt ("I've done so much for you, but you...").

Leaving an unhealthy relationship necessitates a certain level of forward motion in order to break away and chart a new course. When a victim lives with or is subjected to a gaslighter, they begin to lose forward impetus, and inertia sets in. The victim is attempting to break free from the pattern of emotional abuse. Nonetheless, many wonder that they will ever be free, or that they deserve to be free.

Of course, this is a worst-case scenario of gaslighting. And, like with most things in life, there are a variety of gaslighting perpetrators. From this end of the spectrum, where the manipulation is deliberate, to the other end, where the gaslighting may be unintentional. You could, for example, gaslight your own family (with what seems to be noble intentions). If your daughter approaches you with a negative attitude about her homework, you might tell her that she has always liked schoolwork (since you want her to do it) and that you don't see how she can suddenly dislike completing her. Your intentions may be good, but your daughter, who has never loved schoolwork, begins to question her choices and her assessment of her likes and dislikes. You've just lied to your child, even if you only want the best for her. Your assessment of what is best for her undermines her ability to judge herself. From there, the severity of gaslighting can escalate to you telling your daughter that she should date a certain type of guy because she's always liked that type (even if she doesn't), to convincing her to study a certain degree that she's always wanted (even if she'd rather go do International Aid work).

This type of gaslighting may not be emotionally abusive, but it still denies someone's ability to self-regulation by convincing them they want option A when they want option B. It sows doubt and manipulates the victim into changing who they are to suit your wants; worse, they believe this is how they wanted to be in the first place. In their twisted imaginations, the perpetrator of gaslighting is a buddy who has simply showed them the right path.

Gaslighting is similar to narcissism in many ways, but the two are not interchangeable.

GASLIGHTER CHARACTERISTICS

In our daily lives, the consequences and symptoms of gaslighting may be difficult to discern. Gaslighters operate in the shadows, as opposed to narcissists, who virtually glorify their aberrant behaviour. They concentrate on persuading people to become their puppets. It's all about power and adoration. They want their victims to give them authority (by allowing the gaslighter to govern their lives), and as a result, the victim usually ends up applauding the gaslighter, who has persuaded them that they are commendable. Gaslighters manipulate people by using specific phrases. Here are some of the most prevalent terms they use to attain their goals (Arabia, 2019):

Gaslighters' Catchphrases	What They Imply
"You require assistance."	These comments degrade the victim and establish a position of authority for the gaslighter to assume as the savior. You, the victim, are at fault, and the abuser (gaslighter) is not at all to blame.
"You are simply paranoid, insecure, or jealous."	The gaslighter instils these emotions in you. They make you envious, make you feel insecure, and incite paranoia. A husband who tells his wife she's being insecure about his relationship with a coworker when he spends time away from home on purpose is an example of this. This raises the possibility that he is having an affair while simultaneously dismissing his wife's growing suspicions.
"You're overly sensitive." Stop being so dramatic."	Your reactions or sentiments do not suit the needs of the gaslighter and are hence unimportant.
"You've lost your sense of humour."	Gaslighters may cloak their verbal or physical assault as humour. They might make fun of their partner for being bad in bed, bad with money, and overly sensitive. This becomes a form of banter inside the relationship, nearly brainwashing the victim into believing the nasty comments. When you speak up and point out that these statements are unfair or harsh, they

	try to cover it up by stating it's only a joke and you shouldn't be so serious.
"Stop ruminating on the past. You must let go. "Do not beat a dead horse."	Gaslighters want their victims to forget about their previous abuse so that they can continue to abuse them and discover new ways to manipulate them. They are not achieving their objectives if they have to explain their tactics.
"Stop making things up. I never stated anything like that."	The gaslighter trivializes or muddles your memory by denying events. They make you wonder how you remember things that happened in the past. This has the impact of making you question your grasp on reality, generating a sense of vulnerability, and redirecting your emphasis away from confronting the proof of the abuser's involvement and toward your issue with reality.

Although purposeful gaslighting is more severe than unintentional gaslighting, both are harmful in the sense that they deny the victim's reality and ability to choose.

To fulfil their malicious purposes, gaslighters will employ a plethora of weaponry. The weapon used is decided by the severity of the abuse and whether the gaslighting is purposeful or unintentional. To avoid becoming entangled in the vortex of their drama, abuse, and manipulations, you must be aware of these weapons and take necessary actions to protect your well-being.

CHAPTER TWO

THE GASLIGHTER

THE GASLIGHTER

I ndividuals most notorious for gaslighting are profiled here. This type of emotional abuse is frequently linked to mental diseases like narcissistic personality disorder, borderline personality disorder, and antisocial personality disorder. Problematic characteristics and behaviours persist and are dysfunctional. As a result, these people suffer and inflict suffering on others, upsetting their lives and relationships.

Some individuals may exhibit characteristics that do not fit the requirements for a mental health diagnosis. Almost psychopaths is a useful word for people who aren't quite diagnosable. Almost psychopaths may charm, manipulate, and bully the best of them, but they fall short of having a serious mental disease. Abuse can happen to anyone, but not everyone who abuses has a personality condition.

THE ABUSER'S PROFILE

Gaslighting can be a sign of a variety of personality problems. According to the National Institute of Mental Health, around 9% of adults fit the diagnostic criteria for a personality disorder. Though gaslighting is not a clear indicator of a personality disorder—and many gaslighters do not have a mental health diagnosis—people with (diagnosed or undiagnosed) personality disorders are more prone to engage in gaslighting in many situations. Here, we'll look at gaslighting as a symptom of other, more generally identified personality disorders.

NARCISSISTIC PERSONALITY DISORDER (NPD)

A personality disorder is a group of personality traits that persist across relationships and contexts, producing pain and misery. Individuals with a narcissistic personality disorder frequently exhibit traits such as a grandiose attitude, an excessive need for admiration, a lack of empathy and insight, a constant need for praise, a belief that they are special and deserving of special treatment, coercive and manipulative behaviours, and a proclivity to bully others to get their way.

Those with this personality disorder take advantage of others, manipulating and exploiting those around them. Gaslighting is a tactic used by narcissists to retain their sense of superiority by putting others in a position of powerlessness. Many politicians and CEOs have narcissistic tendencies. These power people may employ gaslighting to enrage their supporters or silence their detractors, pursuing their objectives at the expense of others.

PERSONALITY DISORDER WITH BORDERLINE PERSONALITY

At its heart, borderline personality disorder is defined by heightened emotional reactivity, strong fear of rejection, instability in interpersonal relationships, and a sense of emptiness. This illness is also characterised by a proclivity to go between idealising and depreciating loved ones, drawing them closer and driving them away.

Borderline personality disorder patients will go to tremendous measures to escape real or imagined desertion, including threatening to kill themselves if their spouse attempts to leave. They may employ gaslighting in order to make others feel responsible for the gaslighter's well-being. In this situation, gaslighting is less about attempting to influence another person and more about meeting the borderline person's own need to feel secure.

OTHER SOCIOPATHIC CONDITIONS

Those suffering from antisocial personality disorder and psychopathy are also prone to be the perpetrators of gaslighting. Antisocial personality disorder, often known as sociopathy, is defined by a disdain for or violation of others' rights. Individuals who are sociopaths do not conform to societal norms. They are more inclined to gaslight through deception or lying, and they may target damaging conduct at strangers rather than close ones.

Although the phrases are sometimes used interchangeably, the strength and targeting of sociopathic and psychopathic traits differ. Sociopathic people are less likely to actively target those closest to them, but psychopathic people are as likely to hurt family, friends, or strangers. Psychopathic people are similarly careless about the repercussions of their acts, but they lack empathy and sorrow. They may relish causing harm to others.

Abusers employ gaslighting to manipulate their victims in a variety of circumstances and types of relationships. Gaslighters have five pathological goals:

DISABLE THE VICTIM'S DISCERNMENT

The victim is left with doubt and bewilderment as a result of gaslighting. Because the victim challenges their own judgement and views, they may find it difficult to distinguish between right and wrong, healthy and unhealthy, and their own perspective from that of their abuser. Victims of gaslighting believe they can't trust themselves to detect the truth of a situation.

KEEP THE VICTIM SILENT

Abuse thrives in the shadows of silence and concealment. Gaslighting can be a powerful strategy for silencing someone by making them doubt their own trustworthiness. Abusers will dilute the impact and reach of their victim's voice by lying and disparaging them. They may persuade the victim that no one will believe them because the victim is such an untrustworthy witness.

CREATE A SENSE OF POSSESSION OVER THE VICTIM

Victims are duped into forsaking their reality and accepting the abuser's version. Gaslighters use "alternative facts" to replace their victims' perceptions with their own. Gaslighters do not regard their victims' perspectives. Instead, they place a premium on feeling powerful, adored, and in command. Abusers bully their victims because they believe they have the right to alter someone else's reality rather than questioning their own.

MAKE FUN OF AND CHASTISE THE VICTIM

Victims may be degraded and devalued by gaslighters who portray the victim's emotional response to abuse as childish or immature. Chastising a victim for reacting to provocation implies that it is the victim's responsibility, not the abuser's. Abusers may also humiliate their victims by exaggerating the victim's accomplishments or successes. The gaslighter may scold the victim for feeling proud, implying that if the victim worked hard enough, they would have something to show for their efforts that would be worthy of their pride.

LEGITIMIZE THEIR APPROACH TO THE VICTIM

Gaslighting is a technique that can be used to persuade the victim that the perpetrator's abusive behaviour is justified. As they lose faith in their own abilities, they become increasingly reliant on and accepting of the gaslighter's reality. When a victim believes they are deserving of the treatment they are receiving, they are less likely to oppose or confront problematic behaviours. Furthermore, the gaslighter may convince oneself that they are acting harshly for the good of the victim and that this treatment is justified.

WRITING PRACTICE

Gaslighting is an efficient kind of emotional abuse because it methodically undermines the victim's confidence, autonomy, and self-efficacy. The five objectives identified to give the gaslighter more control over their victim. What steps have the gaslighter(s) in your life taken to achieve these aims in your relationship? Write about your encounters with each of their five objectives.

A GASLIGHTER'S COMMON PHRASES

Several frequent gaslighting expressions are listed below. Put a tick in the box next to any that sound familiar.

☐ "You purposefully misconstrued what I said." This term blames the victim for not being able to read the gaslighter's mind, and it indicates that the victim misunderstood the gaslighter's "innocent" aim.

- "You know how I feel about it, and you did it anyway, therefore it's your fault that I reacted the way I did." This statement implies that the victim provoked the gaslighter, justifying their abusive actions in return.
- "That didn't happen." Denying a victim's memories and experiences causes them to become confused and disoriented. Gaslighters also cast doubt on victims by rejecting occurrences or pretending to have no recollection of them.
- "You sound insane." Victims experience self-doubt and anxiety when they are told that their feelings or views are insane.
- "You're attempting to perplex me." This accusation reverses the abuser's and victim's positions, putting the genuine victim on the defence.
- "I'm not sure what you're talking about." Claiming that you don't understand a victim's concern implies that their experience is so out of the ordinary that it's incomprehensible. The sufferer then wonders if they are hallucinating or if their recollection is twisted.
- "You're remembering it incorrectly." This statement implies that the victim's memories and perceptions are untrustworthy, casting doubt on their judgement.
- "I'm only being harsh on you because I adore you." Victims are encouraged to be grateful and pardoned by using this phrase. Abusers assert that they believe in "tough love" or "telling it like it is," regardless of the consequences for the victim.

RECOGNIZING GASLIGHTING BEHAVIOR

Now that you're aware of the warning signs and objectives of gaslighting, you'll be better equipped to avoid falling victim to it in the future. It can be difficult to look back on your history and see the manipulation in a relationship you once thought was love. You may be wondering why you couldn't see through the manipulation at the time, and why you had to go through so much suffering before realising what was going on. You may feel wounded, broken, or foolish as a result of your victimisation. Be kind with yourself. Being targeted by an abusive personality is not a defect in your character.

Victims are targeted for one of two reasons: vulnerability or desirability. Some gaslighters seek victims who are ready to put up with bad treatment and aggressive behaviour. They target people who wish to be viewed as nice and easy to get along with; these people are less likely to call out the gaslighter and are more easily persuaded. There is such a thing as being too polite, and gaslighters will use this to influence their victims.

Abusers may also target people who appear to be self-assured, successful, wealthy, or attractive. They are drawn to persons who are strong and self-assured. Manipulators entice people by showering potential victims with affection, praise, and phoney intimacy in a technique known as "love bombing." Once victims are hooked, the gaslighting begins, and abusers begin to erode the trust that brought them to their target in the first place.

A GASLIGHTEE'S PERSONALITY

Is it true that some personality types are more prone to being gaslighted than others? While abusers target victims for a variety of reasons, many victims share similar characteristics. Many gaslightees are people-pleasers, preoccupied with being nice, agreeable, or liked. They are conscientious, concerned with the sentiments of others, and may feel bad if they say "no." Finally, gaslightees are more willing to accept or overlook unpleasant and hurtful behaviour.

Do you fit the profile of a gaslightee? Take the following self-assessment:

SELF-ASSESSMENT OF A GASLIGHTEE

Circle "Often true," "Sometimes true," or "Rarely true" to indicate how true each statement is for you.

1. Disagreeing with someone makes me feel as though I'm "creating drama." I aim to avoid situations like this.

☐ Frequently true
☐ Occasionally true
☐ Rarely true

2. I'm afraid that if I answer "no," I'll hurt someone's feelings.

☐ Frequently true
☐ Occasionally true
☐ Rarely true

3. I value other people's perspectives more than my own.

☐ Frequently true
☐ Occasionally true
☐ Rarely true

4. If I'm doing well and my partner isn't, I feel that my success is affecting them negatively.

☐ Frequently true
☐ Occasionally true
☐ Rarely true

5. I believe I should be able to regulate my emotions better.

☐ Frequently true
☐ Occasionally true
☐ Rarely true

If you replied "frequently true" to more than three questions, you may be more likely to get gaslighted. Remember that your voice and thoughts are important, and it's alright to say "no." You have the right to be treated with dignity.

CHAPTER THRE

NARCISSISTS AND GASLIGHTING

NARCISSISTS AND GASLIGHTING

So, we've established that narcissists have a role in gaslighting, but what do they do? They are massive manipulators who have a huge influence in altering the reality of others. We'll discuss how they deceive others and why narcissists are bad news for many people.

WHAT EXACTLY IS A NARCISSIST?

A narcissist is someone who has a narcissistic personality disorder. Narcissists have an enormously inflated sense of importance, a need for admiration and attention in their relationships, and frequently fail to empathise with others.

Narcissists are only concerned with themselves. They don't care about you or the guy next to you; they're only interested in themselves. They do, however, have a very fragile ego that will break if they are subjected to even the slightest amount of criticism.

Narcissists are textbook manipulators who are difficult to deal with. This personality type causes many problems in several aspects of life, and you may encounter one of these types without even recognising it. Those with narcissistic personality disorder, on the other hand, are typically unhappy in general if they do not receive the praise they seek. They may find that all of their relationships are unsatisfying, and others may dislike being around these people.

So, how did a narcissist enter your life? Others who suffer from this love tend to gravitate toward those who excite them, making them feel special or distinctive, and as a result, their self-esteem improves. They may crave a great deal of admiration and attention and find it difficult to accept even the mildest criticism. They frequently interpret any criticism as a defeat.

They are so envious of your accomplishments that they will attempt to sabotage them. They can, however. This can range from snide achievements about your own success to underhanded comparisons of others.

Gaslighting is also popular among narcissists; however, we'll get to that in a moment. For the time being, let's focus on how they will undermine you. If you do something amazing, they will try to diminish it by claiming it isn't worth it and that you should do better. If the narcissist is a parent, they may compare you to a sibling or another member of the family. They frequently try to diminish anything you do, making you a shambles in response.

It's not good, and narcissists, in general, are solely concerned with themselves. Of course, many times, just a small percentage of people are really narcissists. Still, male narcissists outnumber female narcissists in general, and you'll frequently encounter them while dealing with bosses, coworkers, or even people you may be friends with or date.

But how are these folks able to utilise gaslighting? They do so, however, in a rather devious manner.

GASLIGHTING AND NARCISSISM

Gaslighting is a favourite tactic of narcissists. It's their favourite, most preferred gaslighting tool. Why is this the case? It's because it's the perfect technique to make you think you're insane, to completely undercut what you think is right, and to effectively tell you that your way of thinking is wrong.

Remember, gaslighting is a very cunning way of making you feel as if your reality is so skewed that you question your sanity or even your memory. Their purpose is to prove that they are correct and you are incorrect, and that is all they want from this.

The idea is to make you believe you're insane, which we'll get to in a moment. Other tactics are available to narcissists, but gaslighting is their bread and butter.

"Oh, I didn't say that."

"Oh, you remember it incorrectly. You should have your health checked out."

You're dealing with a Grade A Narcissist if you've ever heard those two words from someone.

Gaslighting is a tactic used by narcissists to conceal the abuse they are inflicting on you. In essence, gaslighting is lying directly to your face with one purpose in mind: to be in control, the focus of attention, and you're nothing.

Every time a narcissist deceives you, they completely destroy your sense of reality, making you think that you are nothing and they are everything.

They want to slowly but steadily break you down. Memory is one of the simplest methods to accomplish this. Why is this the case? They know that if you can't remember things correctly, you won't be able to trust yourself, distorting your vision and reality as a result.

MAKING OTHERS DO WHAT THE NARCISSIST DESIRES

This is done because, most of the time, if you begin to question how a narcissist behaves, they will immediately gaslight you, claiming that it did not happen this way.

You see your narcissist abuser is acting gross and cruel, and you notice them flirting with other girls, for example. They absolutely are, and if you call them out on it, they will quickly deny it, tell you that you're crazy, that you're making stuff up, and that whatever you saw was incorrect.

You know what the reality is deep inside. That the actions you witnessed were correct, but over time, this individual will tell you that you're insane and didn't hear or say what was stated.

You begin to doubt your reality and wonder if you remembered things correctly. Maybe you didn't notice the other individual flirting with the gals. You begin to become deafeningly quiet about it. When, in actuality, your narcissist was doing it, didn't come clean, and now this person is seeing girls, and every time you call them out on it, and their trust and validity, it basically tells you that you're insane and incorrect.

After a while, you give up fighting the narcissist. You notice that every time you fight them, there is no end to it, and the fact that you're continuously informed that you're crazy every time you do isn't helping matters. So, what are you going to do now?

The answer is that most people succumb to their abusers.

Instead of doing what they believe is right, calling out the abuser, and recognising the toxic characteristics, they begin to do what the abuser wants. When you're being gaslighted, you begin to believe that you're wrong and that the narcissist is correct. You've been tricked into believing that the narcissist is the correct person, and you're wrong, rendering your reality meaningless.

If you allow this to continue, you are fueling the other person's need for narcissism. You may begin to view things incorrectly, and often to the point where you swear it was that way, but maybe your stuff is gone because the narcissist hides it, and then they claim that you're reckless and untrustworthy. They will then tell you that you are wrong and insane, and they will begin to convince others that you are insane.

They will even set others against you in order to isolate you. They will frequently try to pit you against others so that you dump them and the only person in your life is the narcissist. They will fabricate lies, and you can only trust the one who is gaslighting you. When, in fact, the person who is gaslighting you is the last person you should believe! Deceivers may not realise how dangerous they are, or they may. They will begin to make you doubt even the oddest strangers. You may begin to dismiss someone's activities as innocuous, but the gaslighted will label it flirting, and you will soon begin to attack anyone who comes at you.

Have you ever seen something like this? Perhaps you've had a similar experience. You'll hear about how someone was looking at you the wrong way, and you'll grow tired and irritated with the other person, and those connections will eventually fall apart because you don't trust them. When, in truth, it is the narcissist who cannot be trusted since they are the one who has led you astray.

A narcissist will practically hurt everyone in your life, pitting you against your friends and family in order to distract you from what the narcissist is doing, which is feeding you poisonous lies.

It's a messy scenario that most of us don't want to deal with.

Yes, a narcissist will engage in gaslighting. It's the narcissist's go-to tool because they know they can bend others to their will, making it very easy to manipulate them, which is why many narcissists will smile at you with a warm, fake smile and then stab you in the back whenever you turn around or turn your family and friends against you, so the only person you can rely on is the narcissist themselves.

CHAPTER FOUR

EFFECTS OF GASLIGHTING

EFFECTS OF GASLIGHTING

Gaslighting is a crazy-making effect that can lead to exploitation, which can be difficult to detect at times. The objective of the individual utilising gaslighting is to gradually and methodically erode the victim's self-confidence to the point where they are unable to act freely. In the end, the victim is transformed into a robot that only obeys the manipulator's commands.

The victim can suffer significant emotional harm as a result of gaslighting. When a person is subjected to gaslighting for an extended period of time, they lose their sense of self-identity, begin to question their judgement, and second-guess themselves.

Gaslighting can cause emotional and mental problems in the victim. Anxiety can be exacerbated by self-doubt and perplexity, and anxiety can lead to depression, post-traumatic stress disorder, and codependency.

The repercussions of gaslighting can be harmful to the victim; these effects do not occur all at once; instead, they occur in three stages: disbelief, defence, and melancholy. Before we go into these levels, let's look at the negative effects of gaslighting on victims.

CONFUSION

Gaslighting works when the victim is unaware of it, and the narcissist's repeated use of gaslighting tactics causes the victim to eventually submit to their will. Doubts sneak into the victims' minds over time, and as the gaslighting intensifies, the victim becomes perplexed by what is going on. They are aware that something is wrong, but they are unable to pinpoint what it is.

As long as the victims are in close proximity to the narcissist, it is a never-ending cycle. The victim's vulnerabilities are exploited by the narcissist, resulting in confusion. Because they alternate between acts of violence and acts of love, narcissists keep their victims constantly second-guessing what they throw at them.

The narcissists rip down victims' piece by piece, making them more and more unstable, and victims eventually begin to rely on them for comfort and guidance as confusion takes its toll on victims mentally and physically.

Confusion among victims eventually leads to isolation, as victims are unsure how the situation came to be in the first place.

LACK OF SELF-BELIEF

When a person falls prey to a gaslighting narcissist, their confidence begins to crumble, and they may begin to second-guess themselves, leading to a heightened sense of self-doubt. Every decision will now be accompanied with the mental query, "What if I...?"

Victims begin to live in fear of doing the wrong thing because they are now sensitive to the narcissist's incessant projection, blame, falsehoods, and humiliation. They wonder themselves, "Am I too sensitive...?" as a result of looking up to the narcissist for approval before acting. And, as a result of their nervousness, individuals frequently make blunders in their activities.

As time passes, the victim will begin to exhibit indicators of low confidence; they will find it difficult to say a simple thank you when complimented. This occurs as a result of the gaslighting victim's unconscious emotional damage: the victim will reject a good perspective of themselves because they have unconsciously accepted the reality that they are unworthy of the narcissist.

A victim may find it difficult to maintain eye contact with others because they are frightened that others will see straight through them and point out their shortcomings. The narcissists have succeeded in projecting a portion of themselves onto the victim. Loss of confidence also causes victims to always apologise because they are never doing anything right in the perspective of the narcissist, and they apologise even for the words they utter to avoid further name-calling and humiliation.

INDECISION

As the victim doesn't know what's real and what's imagined, the victim is prone to questioning everything. As a result, the victim finds it difficult to make even the most basic decisions since they no longer know what is "good" and "wrong."

Victims of gaslighting have difficulty making significant decisions, but even simple choices like brushing their teeth have become difficult because they have become entangled in the narcissist's web of illusion and are tied to the narcissist.

This type of link with the narcissist is created out of the victim's fear of losing their sense of self. One aspect of the victim will want to align itself with the narcissist's needs and preferences, while another will try to align itself with the victim's preferences.

Furthermore, the narcissist puts their fear of taking responsibility and the drive for perfection onto the victim, making it difficult to make decisions.

Victims gradually lose their ability to make decisions, until they are unable to make any decisions for themselves. They must now rely on the narcissist for guidance and seek permission from the narcissist to do things.

DISTRUST

As a result of the identical feelings that victims of gaslighting experience, they strive to conceal the fact that mental manipulation is taking place in their lives, and when their family and best friends detect the changes in them, they reject the matter and cover-up, or they avoid the problem.

Victims of gaslighting begin to withhold information from well-meaning others because they are afraid of what will happen if the narcissist finds out. They begin to retreat from society and develop a suspicion of others. Victims of gaslighting not only have difficulty trusting family and friends, but they also progressively doubt their own abilities.

Victims of distrust not only find it difficult to create new friendships and relationships, but they often retreat from friends and family. This effect of gaslighting persists even after the victim has successfully removed the narcissist from their lives, since when they make new friends, they find it difficult to trust and are always wary of connections.

MELAN CHOLY

The victim's happiness and delight will be taken away over time if gaslighting is used on them. Through mental manipulation and emotional abuse, narcissists make their victims fearful, confused, lonely, and miserable.

The sufferers have the impression that they were once a different person, one who was self-assured and carefree. What the victims don't comprehend is that anyone who lives under the relentless oppression of the gaslighting narcissist has the ability to change their personality.

This heinous deed accumulates over time, causing a dramatic personality change in the victims: victims who were formerly peaceful, fun-loving, and their best selves are now depressed as a result of the mental abuse.

After a while, victims of gaslighting develop despair as a result of the repeated betrayal, blame-shifting, cognitive dissonance, and mental manipulation.

Victims experience the impacts of gaslighting in phases, and when they suffer at the hands of a gaslighting narcissist, they will go through three stages: disbelief, defence, and depression. When depression sets in, the victim rejects reality, and the narcissist triumphs.

DISBELIEF IS THE FIRST STAGE.

The victim's first reaction to gaslighting conduct is disbelief. They are perplexed as to what is going on and why the narcissist has suddenly changed their attitude toward them. Of course, narcissists want this because they know the victim will bow to their wishes and allow them to control the victim's reality.

Initially, the narcissist presented the victim with a distorted vision of themselves. In the victim's perspective, a narcissist is a person full of affection, and they would find it difficult to understand that a person who formerly showed them love is now something different.

This first stage is characterised by the victim's complete unawareness. The victim is not aware of the narcissist's use of gaslighting. All they see is that the narcissist who once supported and loved them is now very critical of them, and any attempt to discuss the reason for the change in attitude is blocked or diverted into something unrelated to the reason for the change in attitude, or in worse cases, the attempt to discuss is met with silence.

At this point, love-bombing ceases and nitpicking begins: the victims are taken aback by the narcissist's abrupt change in behaviour. The narcissist was once the perfect person, and now they are a shell of their former self.

At this point, the victim will still be trying to make sense of things and may ascribe the narcissist's sudden change of conduct to another incident in his or her life.

After a while, the narcissist may appear to be healthy and okay in the victim's eyes, but this is just temporary, as the narcissists will return with greater vigour, and their negative behaviour will now become a never-ending cycle.

This is also the stage at which the narcissist begins to confuse the victim's thinking by their acts and statements. Later, at this point, the victim begins to rely on the narcissist for a sense of reality.

SECOND STAGE: DEFENSE

At this point, the victim retains the ability to fight and defend oneself against the gaslighting manipulation. At this point, the narcissist is gaslighting using hidden threats, triangulation, and name-calling.

The narcissist is working hard to convince the victim that they are insane at this time, but a portion of the victim is resisting this while another part has accepted that the victim is insane.

At this point, the gaslighting tactics are beginning to operate, but the victim retains control over a little portion of their mind. At this point, gaslighting has worn away a section of the victim's psyche, and the victim begins to mentally weaken and succumb.

In any event, the narcissist's gaslighting is beginning to achieve what it is supposed to do: scare the victim by instilling self-doubt and shame in them. After a while, the victim loses their perception of the real world as well as their sense of self as a result of emotional injury. They become disoriented and unable to rely on their memories. The victim may begin to feel embarrassed, and after a while, the victim may believe they are in grave danger.

Psychologists believe that nature has built-in coping mechanisms for us to use from birth when we believe we are about to be destroyed.

One of these coping techniques is known as "Stockholm Syndrome," in which the victim adapts to the traumatic situation by instinctively reverting to childhood patterns of behaviour and bonds with their abuser like they did with their mother when they were younger.

Another coping method is "Cognitive Dissonance," which occurs when the victim attempts to justify the narcissist's actions.

Victims defend themselves by doing two things in response to gaslighting:

They rationalise the abusive narcissist's actions, and as a result, they experience cognitive dissonance. This is a sense of discomfort that arises when a person's mind has contradicting concepts or beliefs at the same time. As a defence against the narcissist's gaslighting, they resort to childhood behaviours. They begin to bond with the narcissist in this regressive mode, much as they did with their mothers when they were kids. Out of dread of the narcissist, this is done unconsciously.

DEPRESSION IS THE THIRD STAGE.

Gaslighting has had its full effect at this point, and the victim has become a shell of their former self. They begin to believe they are unable to make decisions; they are unable to deal with reality; and they shrink into depression.

By this point, the victim can hardly recognise themselves, and they are gradually transforming into a shadow of their former self, living inside a war zone where they are physically and emotionally controlled. The victim begins to avoid people, places, or thoughts and loses interest in things that provide them with satisfaction and delight. They also begin to relive previous events.

They begin to have difficulties concentrating on their tasks at this time, and they feel despondent. They begin to believe that they can no longer perform anything correctly, that they cannot trust their minds, and they withdraw into sadness.

CHAPTER FIVE

GASLIGHTING IN RELATIONSHIPS

GASLIGHTING IN RELATIONSHIPS

Most individuals, I believe, expect or have experienced true narcissism from a love partner, yet this toxic connection can develop between any two people. Once two people develop a power dynamic, one of them can take advantage of the other.

Perhaps you've seen a buddy have a poor relationship that made you roll your eyes and worry how much longer you'd have to put up with the jerk. You may have been in a horrible relationship and heard sighs of relief when you left. Outside of an unhealthy relationship, it is simple to point fingers at someone else's suffering, yet we all fall victim to the same tactics, especially when they may creep up on us from behind. Do you know when to go on the offensive with an employer or a parent? What about a friend who always appears to get their way, even though all they want to do is cause a commotion? Can our siblings take advantage of our affection as well?

We need to understand what a narcissistic gaslighting factor looks like in all relationships so that we can label them as toxic. When we understand the truth behind a tough relationship, we can find strategies to distance ourselves from the individual who is causing us harm.

I'd like to look into some of the unique relationships in our life that can influence how we live and love. My goal is to get everyone talking freely about these circumstances so that we don't laugh at or dismiss someone who is in agony. Instead, we might approach them as knowledgeable friends or family members and assist them in seeing the reality.

A PARENT OR CARETAKER

Most of the people I know had parents who hoped their children would eventually leave home. These children grow up to further their education, launch enterprises, fall in love, and create their own lives.

We presume that the majority of parents want their children to grow up to be healthy, productive people. We wish the same for anyone living in a foster family or with relatives who have taken the role of Mom and Dad. Parenting isn't easy; we're all aware that it may become abusive or hazardous, but it's more difficult to perceive the gaslighting that a parent offers a child.

When a mother, father, or caregiver engages in gaslighting, the goal is to make the victim feel inadequate, but in a more basic sense than a romantic partner might. Because children's lives are less nuanced than adults', abuse follows suit.

My mother was always nitpicking my neatness, saying, "You call this a tidy room?" No matter how many hours I spent organising, scrubbing, or making my bed, none of it ever fulfilled her expectations. My As in school were also inadequate since education was "dumbed down to make fools feel smart."

Unrealistic tasks and academic expectations are simple methods for parents to put their children down. I had no defence as a child. My mother must have known what she was talking about—after all, she had already graduated from college. Her room was as tidy as a pin. Who was I to interrogate her? A narcissistic parent relies on dynamic gaslighting to keep the abuse going. These parents play the role of the hero in their child's storey, as if to say, "I'm here to tell you the truth and show you what the world is truly like."

Adults are not questioned by children. Mom and dad are physically larger, older, and ostensibly smarter than you. Because a youngster has no bruises or markings to show for the abuse, it is far more difficult for others to notice the damage, and a child is reluctant to disclose these cutting remarks. They are most likely unaware that they are being abused. To a child, the behaviour quickly becomes normal, and they assume that everyone else's mother and father behave similarly.

Several strategies are used to increase acceptance over time. By intruding their child's social life, narcissist parents ensure that they have no refuge to turn to. My mother would frequently read my AIM notes from pals aloud in hilarious voices, attempting to make my friends' words appear stupid. Unfortunately, it worked. I stopped checking in and remained silent, giving her the opportunity to point out that she had an unpopular son.

I made the mistake of asking a friend over for dinner one day in third grade. My mum put up a show like I'd never seen before, so I say mistake. She came out with a platter of cookies, joined us in our video game, and interrogated my friend about his mother. My friend was racing for the door before I knew it, uneasy with my "strange mom," who seemed to think he had come to see her.

"We'll come to your house next time," I promised. But I didn't see him much after that. Of course, my mother pointed out that it was my fault that I didn't know how to entertain a visitor.

"You could learn a lot from me," she said, crossing her arms and looking down at me. I agreed, exhausted.

I recall wondering if my mother would apologise after she knew my friend didn't want to see me anymore. A narcissist, on the other hand, never apologises, especially to a youngster. I hoped she'd say it in secret, where no one else could hear, and that she'd pledge not to repeat her deep apologies. Even back then, I could tell that it was difficult for my mother to accept a mistake. As an adult, I met many people who grew up in homes like mine. One or both of their parents barred them from making friends, made them feel stupid, or intruded on their personal space.

CHILDREN

I'm saddened by the parent gaslighter since our parents should be our lighthouse in a dark, uncertain world. Rather than assisting us in navigating school, first loves, or new careers, a narcissistic parent sees their offspring drifting further away from home and gaining autonomy. That is a terrible prospect for a self-centered mother or father. Unfortunately, the condition can also be reversed. Some sons and daughters take advantage of their parents' needs as they age and begin to rely on their offspring for support. I was fortunate to meet Marcia, a lawyer who focuses on the rights of the elderly. She takes on elder abuse cases, which frequently involve the victim's children, the church, or others responsible with keeping them safe.

"It's heartbreaking," she admitted to me. "True narcissists will go to any length to make their parents appear insane or helpless." It makes no difference if the mother or father in question is lucid, healthy, and completely capable. Their children strive constantly to persuade anybody who will listen that they are unable to drive, cannot be left alone, or are gradually losing their marbles.

"I had one son who frequently hid things from his mother, then shook his head at her as if she were a foolish child when she couldn't locate anything." She even found him stowing her money in an unusual location one day, but when she confronted him, he threatened to place her in a home. She became so terrified that she ended up apologising to him, despite the fact that he was at fault.

"Another woman brought her children to court because they made a big deal about how inept she'd become at their church." The church had a programme to help take care of elderly parishioners, but it was just for those who couldn't clean or cook for themselves. Her children appeared to believe that if she was a recipient of the charity, it would be simpler to take over her estate before she died.

"Of course, there are countless stories of people physically abusing their parents in order to gain control of their bank accounts, get them out of their homes, keep them dependent, or all three." It's quite disturbing. The individuals who owe these people everything turn on them seemingly instantaneously, despite the fact that they've clearly had narcissistic tendencies for years."

Ray told me about his two sons, who were growing up before his eyes. They morphed from two kind young men to scheming middle-aged villains. "I'll never be able to get over that." I believed I had the most wonderful family on the planet. I dug through my recollections for evidence that the seeds of their behaviour were planted someplace, but I honestly can't think of anything that motivated them to do this.

"At first, they came around all the time and frequently inquired about my bills. 'Are you paying your electricity bill, Dad? 'Do you have gas?' Yes, I said, the bank had done it all for me. What was the point of caring? They didn't live in my house. I had to send them away a couple of times just to get some peace and quiet.

"After their billing strategy failed, they began alerting me about various types of banking fraud." They told me storey after storey of people calling elderly folks and duping them into sending money to people under false pretences. I informed them that I had educated myself and that the community centre had a particular course on fraud avoidance. They insisted, however, that I exercise extreme caution.

"The phone rang one day while I was sitting at home alone." It was someone claiming to be from the bank and requesting my account information. My money had been compromised. I've learned not to offer personal information over the phone. So I performed what I had learned in class and hung up before dialling the number again. By the way, that's a clever trick.

"I called again, and to my surprise, someone answered." It was my own son! I screamed at him. I honestly assumed he was conniving individuals like me and had contacted me by mistake. Maybe he had one of those dial-by-phone gadgets. I was so enraged when he hung up on me that I shook in my chair. I needed to go for a long walk to calm down.

"He strolled into the house with his brother the next day, a big smile on his face." I approached him, my finger in his face, and said,

'Do you want to say something to me?'

"He shrugged and pretended to be deafeningly deafeningly deaf 'What's going on, Dad?' 'Did anything happen?'

"I became so enraged and broken up inside that I began to cry." That little phoney had the audacity to wrap his arms around me as if he was sorry for me. I shoved him away, and he made a huge show of collapsing, but even his brother didn't believe him.

"I attempted to speak with my eldest about the phone event, but he appeared sceptical." He gave me this look and asked, 'Are you sure, Dad?' 'You're not perplexed about anything?' Oh, that's it. I told them both to keep away from me. Then I called my bank and informed them that I suspected my children of attempting to steal from me. I wasn't sure how, but I needed some type of security on my account.

"The woman at the bank mentioned how they'd come to see her and inquired what they should do if they needed to take over my accounts." That tore at my heart. I'd hoped it was just my younger kid trying to con me, but both? Everything seemed to crumble around me.

"I haven't spoken to them in months, and I have no plans to make amends with them." Suspicious of your children is a terrible thing to do. What if I develop Alzheimer's disease? What if I trip and fall? I can only think how pleased they'd be. It's dreadful. It's lethal."

It's difficult to fathom a parent being cruelly abused by their children, but it occurs more frequently than you might believe. According to the National Care Planning Council, one out of every 10 seniors is assaulted at home, and around 90 percent of those cases go unreported. Older family members are frequently convinced that if they complain about their families, they would lose access to transportation or financial resources.

In the case of those who live with narcissists, they are most likely correct.

CHAPTER SIX

SYMPTOMS OF GASLIGHTING

SYMPTOMS OF GASLIGHTING

So, what are some of the symptoms of gaslighting that you may notice, feel, or be wary of? Here, we'll go over the signs of gaslighting that you should be aware of.

FALSEHOODS

This is one to be cautious of at all times. The person who is gaslighting you enjoys telling lies. After all, they are well aware that these are outright lies. But why are they so obvious? Essentially, this is establishing the standard against which they will work. For example, if you begin to believe their lies, you may begin to give in. You will begin to doubt whether or not what they say is true. You know it's a falsehood, but every time you try to counter it, they either completely disregard what you say or blame you.

It is frequently accompanied by denial. They will deny everything until the day they die, even if they are aware that you have proof. They will frequently act as if they would do something, and then do it, but when caught, they will entirely deny it. Even if you have proof, they will say you're making it up, insane, and lying.

But are you telling the truth?

 Nope.

They will, however, fight you tooth and nail until you give up. The goal that they have in mind is to ensure that they are in charge, and the purpose of this is complete control, so that your reality is entirely tarnished so that you will accept all that they say. Even if it isn't accurate.

THEY'LL USE YOUR FAVORITE THINGS AS AMMO

This is common when dealing with a child who has been gaslighted about who his or her parent is. They enjoy using children as ammo. They could do this with other items as well. They exploit your love for your pets as ammo. If you have a close family, they'll make sure you know how important it is to them, and it'll be one of the first things they select to attack.

If you have a family, they may tell you that you shouldn't be too close to them, or that your family is sympathetic to your situation. When it comes to children, they'll tell you that you're not deserving of them and that you shouldn't have them.

They intend to attack you behind the belt. They will target your negative traits and tell you that you stink, that you do everything wrong, and that you are useless.

What motivates them to act in this manner? They most likely intend to take you down a notch or two until you accept whatever your abuser says as fact. You will begin to wonder if you are because they will attack all of your vulnerable places, even if you do not believe they will.

YOU'RE EXHAUSTED JUST TALKING TO THEM.

If you feel this way when you're talking to somebody, you're probably being gaslit. This is why gaslighting is so pernicious; they know it will wear you down over time.
The comments will be snarky, they'll say things here and there, it'll all be devious, but the purpose is to gradually erode your fortitude, to tear you down.
What's worse, it works.

Even those with great strength, power, and talent, as well as those who are self-aware of their behaviours and sentiments, can get drawn into this trap, which is why it is so terrifying. It's similar to the frog in a frying pan simile.
Have you ever heard of it? The comparison is that frogs are placed in a frying pan, but the heat is gradually increased, to the point where the frog will not realise until it's burnt to a crisp—at which time it's too late.
The deadliest aspect of gaslighting is that you may not even realise you're being abused in this manner until it's too late, which is why many abusers will continue to do so for years.

WORDS AND ACTIONS DO NOT MATCH.

Remember the adage "actions speak louder than words"? When dealing with someone who enjoys gaslighting, you should pay attention to their actions rather than their words. They will do things that are often diametrically opposed to what they say.
"Oh, sweetie, I would never talk to her and hurt you."— She runs away and is seen with other girls.
"I adore you, dear"—Will entirely dismiss your life.
"I love you and want you to live your own life." —Will confiscate their daughter's clothing and other components of her fashion.
This is especially often with abusive lovers or abusive parents, who will say one thing and then do another, and they frequently end up making it so that they are not doing what they should be doing.
Of course, the goal here is to perplex you and make you wonder if this person has a true self and if they are who they claim to be.

POSITIVITY IS THROWN AT YOU TO CONFUSE YOU.

This is something that many people would be unaware of. They will occasionally throw positive at you to confuse you. They'll be terrible bastards to you, always making you feel like nothing, putting you down and making you feel horrible, will tell outright lies and say you're insane, but every now and then, they'll sprinkle a little positive reinforcement to try to confuse you.

They will cut you down and tell you that you are worthless, but will then randomly laud you for your activities.

Why would they do such a thing? Wouldn't it be better if you were simply dismissed? No, because the purpose is to perplex you and make you feel uneasy.

They urge you to believe that the abuser "isn't all that horrible, right?" and you begin to let the abuser get away with things because they are occasionally nice to you. They will frequently attempt to make you question your reality, and it will work. When you look at what you were praised for, you can typically connect it back to how it benefited the gaslighted.

This is especially true in partnerships characterised by narcissistic gaslighting. You have a narcissistic mother, are continuously belittled, ripped down, and are frequently made to be nothing. But every now and then, you get a slight glimmer of "hey, you're not garbage" from them. This is only because you did something that made them happy or was beneficial to them. They will frequently try to toss in a little bit of their own two cents, claiming that it was them that helped out, and that's why you were so successful.

YOU'RE PERPLEXED AND WEAK.

The name of the game is perplexity. Why is this the case? Confusion, on the other hand, is how you weaken a person.

They understand that people seek stability. They desire the status quo and the normalcy that comes with it. They, on the other hand, seek to completely uproot that and make you doubt everything that happens. And, of course, we have a natural tendency to look at the entity that will make you feel more stable and see them as someone to whom they should turn when things get difficult.

But who is the person to whom they turn? You guessed it, it's the one who's deceiving them.

They want you to be perplexed, with nowhere else to turn, and the only solution being your gaslighting. They don't want you to feel stable and secure, and they'll do all in their power to make sure you don't.

PROJECTION, PROJECTION, PROJECTION!

These sorts' bread and butter is projection. We'll go into this a little more later, but they do experience the cognitive dissonance and projection that most abusive and nasty individuals do.

They will accuse you of cheating, stealing goods, and, more often than not, of doing something illegal.

When you begin to be accused, you will discover yourself, and as you attempt to defend yourself, it will become about you. They may even try to perplex you by claiming that you are the one who is doing everything, causing you to develop a guilt complex.

But who is the true cheater in this situation? Who is the true abusor? The gaslighting, you guessed it.

They will start blaming you right away, with the intention of taking the blame and putting it somewhere else. They are the ones who are deceiving. But every time you talk to them about it or confront them about it, it is promptly returned to you, one for one.

OTHERS ARE WORKING AGAINST YOU.

Don't assume they're simply after you and want to crush you at this stage. No, they are skilled at influencing those they know will be near them at all times, and they will use them against you.

For example, if your narcissistic mother is gaslighting you, chances are she has a "golden child" who can do no wrong, who is faultless, and who she can easily control and use against you. They will say things like "the other person knows you're wrong," or "you're worthless and can't be trusted." However, they may not have even informed others about you, or that other person may have never said it, but they are lying and will continue to lie.

Gaslighters love to use this method to confuse you about who is a friend or adversary and who you can trust. Of course, the idea is for you to recognise that there is no one and that you must be with the gaslighted.

Of course, this gives them exactly what they want, as well as more control. They want you to return to the gaslighted, and you'll notice that there is a lot that happens as a result of this, and you may feel as if your family hates you.

Sometimes narcissistic mothers or stepmothers will turn one side of the family against you and claim that this person despises you and never wants to see you. That, however, is not the case. When you reconnect with them, they may claim that was never the case and that they were mistaken.

You can thank your gaslighted for that, of course.

YOU HAVE A CRAZY FEELING

They may tell you directly that you're insane, or they may tell others that you're insane. Because it is done in such a dismissive manner, this is one of their key tools. They will occasionally state flatly that this person is insane, that they should not be trusted, and that you should not listen to them. When they say this, they know you're not going to question it.

Of course, if the other person questions it and asks you, they won't believe you because they know that when you say the gaslighting is abusive, it's out of your control, and it's a very good technique.

IS ENVIOUS AND BELIEVES THAT EVERYONE IS LYING.

If you see that the other person is jealous of the person who has been gaslighted, or that everyone else is a liar, it's time to get out of there and realise what you're dealing with. The idea is that if you tell the person who is being mistreated that everyone else is a liar, guess what happens next? Of course, it makes you question your reality! You'll never know someone who has the courage (or recklessness) to do anything like this, and clearly, you're gaslighted, so it has to be real, right? No, it isn't. They will claim that everyone is lying, that everyone else is wrong, and that the gaslighted is the only one who has the correct knowledge

CHAPTER SEVEN

PHRASES USED BY NARCISSISTS IN

GASLIGHTING

PHRASES USED BY NARCISSISTS IN GASLIGHTING

When a narcissist is attempting to use the gaslighting tactic on you, they may say a variety of things. Understanding what is going on immediately in front of your eyes might be aided by becoming acquainted with the many types of language that they may employ. When dealing with a gaslighting narcissist, knowledge is power.

If you have or are in a relationship with a narcissist, you may recognise many of these expressions. Know that you are not alone and that you can recover from the abuse you have experienced or may continue to experience. Recognizing specific phrases used by narcissists might empower you to take action against the abuse they pour at you on a daily basis.

Here are 100 various questions, comments, and phrases that narcissists may use to deceive you:

- Why are you acting irrationally?
- You are continuously making up stories in your thoughts. You should definitely get assistance.
- I don't do anything if I believe it is wrong. You're always on the defensive.
- You behave like a child.
- Why are you behaving so childishly?
- Your communication abilities are severely weak. This isn't an argument; it's a discussion.
- I'm not attempting to persuade you to change.
- Isn't there always something going on with you? You're insane, aren't you?
- I wouldn't be cruel to you if you didn't make me furious on purpose.
- It's easy to understand why people dislike you.
- I assumed you were a wonderful person, but your behaviour has shown me that I was mistaken.
- Simply get over it.
- I'm not going to play your games.
- If you chose to tell people about me, your life will be a living misery.
- You're a moron, aren't you?
- People refer to me as the smart one in this relationship because of responses like that.
- If you keep doing this, you'll lose me.
- I'll just suck up to make sure people prefer me to you. Don't you realise you can't beat me?
- You are constantly making a fool of yourself. I feel bad for you, man.
- That's correct, and you're more holy than thou. Oh, you sad thing.
- Stop acting as if you're a victim.
- When you act like this, it's clear to see why I avoid you.
- What exactly do you mean? Everyone else thinks I'm a lovely man, but I'm not.
- If you continue to put me down, I will avoid you forever.
- You're probably wondering why I drink (or do drugs, depending on the situation).
- I always feel bad when you're around.
- Do you pay attention to yourself? You come across as insane. You're venting your frustrations on me.
- What do you mean I'm attempting to exert authority over you? That is completely absurd. I simply care about what is best for you.
- Why do you seem to have a problem all the time? You can never be really content, can you?
- You will miss me because I am the best thing that has ever happened to you
- I love you more than anyone else could ever love you.
- Can't you see that you're the source of all of our problems? It's entirely your responsibility.
- Why does everything put you in a poor mood or cause you pain? You do need to find something to moan about on a daily basis, don't you?
- Is it enjoyable for you to be moody all of the time? It had to be because it is so consistent.
- Except for me, no one else loves you. You have no right to try to control me.

- My worry is not for your children.
- Everyone agrees that you're in the wrong here. You're insane.
- What exactly do you mean? I never stated anything like that. Stop being such a wimp.
- I'm always aware of what you're thinking. It's written all over you, I swear.
- Why can't you just listen for a minute?
- Remove that expression from your face before I do it for you. You're a scumbag.
- You're completely clueless.
- Stop being concerned about everything. You're an oddball, aren't you?
- You will be sorry if you continue to talk about me. There is no one better than me for you.
- Who wants someone like you?
- I am far smarter than commoners like you.
- Can't you see how vital I am? I'm working on huge projects, and all you do is paperwork.
- Stop disturbing me with your nonsense. Get out if you don't do it my way.
- Men are more powerful than women.
- I understand why you act this way; you're unstable.
- If you'd only listen to me, I'd have the answer you're looking for. Just sit back and wait to see what happens next.
- It's no surprise your kids are messed up; they're just like you. Have you ever wondered if you have bipolar disorder?
- Why do you always approach me at the most inconvenient times? You always act as if I'm doing anything wrong. Your friends are all making fun of you behind your back.
- Except for me, no one likes you.
- Isn't there always something wrong with you?
- Will you abandon me? Okay, you're never going to be brave enough to do it. Are you delusory?
- What friends do you have? You don't have any.
- Why would anyone want to be your friend? You've certainly gained weight, haven't you?
- You will never discover another love like the one I offer you.
- There is no one better out there for you than me.
- Good luck finding someone to put up with you if you leave me. You're not going to make it without me.
- You must be insane to believe I said that. Perhaps you should consult with a psychiatrist.
- I am the only person who would fall in love with someone like you. Stop bothering me.
- You can't take a joke, can you? Why are you always so judgmental? Get off my back, please. I was preoccupied.
- You need to mature.
- Can't you see that you began this problem, not me? Can't you just go on?
- Why do you get so worked up over trivial matters?

Each of these phrases or comments is intended to manipulate. They can be found in the everyday lives of those who are in relationships with narcissists. They may appear to be fairly ordinary things to say during an argument, but realistically, if you are in a good relationship with someone who cares about you, they will not say such things.

The toxicity of speaking such things will undoubtedly have an effect on anyone. They can have the same effect on you no matter how bright you are. When we are constantly taught the same thing, we begin to believe it. Every time we hear it, a little more of our self-worth is eroded. Recognizing these statements early in a connection or relationship might help you prevent the negative consequences they can have on a person.

When dealing with a parent or a family member, it can be a little more difficult to get away from. This is especially true if you are still living in their home. There isn't much you can do except grasp what's going on so that the consequences aren't as severe. Remind yourself of what they're doing and locate a secure place to vent your rage. You must keep in mind that it is doubtful that you would be able to change the narcissist's tendencies.

The only thing you can do is defend yourself and comprehend what they are attempting to get ultimate control. We already discussed how crucial awareness may be while dealing with a narcissist. When listening to these types of comments and expressions, this is accurate. Allow yourself to remain in the present moment and observe what is going on. The things they're stating are almost certainly false. They are simply attempting to persuade you to accept their point of view in order to gain control over you and your connection with them. They feel nice because they make you feel horrible.

The narcissist lives in a distorted universe in which everything revolves around them. They are utterly self-centered and are unconcerned about the hurt their remarks are inflicting you. Knowing their strategies and realising that what they say is not true will help to keep your self-esteem from plummeting. When dealing with a narcissist, you should always consult with trusted persons in your life. Depending on how much damage your narcissistic partner has inflicted, you may feel as if they don't understand or don't care.

This is not correct. People who have loved and cared for you will continue to love and care for you. They are most likely concerned about you and would encourage you to contact them. If you are experiencing gaslighting, having a healthy support system is crucial to preserving your sense of self and sanity. It's difficult to deal with someone who constantly digs against you. Many individuals will not realise what is happening until it is too late, and they have been victims of these tactics for far too long.

It is critical to remember that you should never cease trusting the people you trusted before entering into a relationship with a narcissist. They will be able to give you a different perspective on things, and they will most likely perceive what is going on for what it is. Even if you can't see it, that doesn't mean it isn't taking place. Because the effects of gaslighting make it difficult for the person in the scenario to be mindful and aware of what is going on, relying on others who love you to help guide you is a wise decision, even if it is difficult to see it from their perspective.

If you haven't been in a narcissistic relationship for very long, it's much easier to notice these behaviours happening, and you're much more likely to be able to stop them before they cause you serious harm. It is difficult to be conscious of what you are dealing with, but it is also feasible. When you start hearing these types of comments and words, the best thing you can do is cut ties with the individual who is saying them to you. If that is not possible, you should concentrate on anchoring yourself in your convictions and understanding that you are a person worthy of love and respect, regardless of what is said to you.

The phrases and comments we've listed are some of the most popular among narcissists that use the gaslighting approach, but there are many more. Your lovers, friends, and family members should not treat you in this manner. We should be kind and compassionate to one another. The words we use matter a lot, and those who truly care about you would never use such cruel language that is insulting and damaging to a person's mind. Stay tough and defend yourself against people who speak to you in this manner to guarantee that you always know your worth and are in healthy relationships worth your time.

CHAPTER EIGHT

STOPPING GASLIGHTING

STOPPING GASLIGHTING

G aslighting is a harmful event in our lives, and counteracting its effects may be far more difficult than just saying, "Avoid it." If you are already married to a gaslighter or your boss is a narcissist who manipulates you, it is not as simple as seeking a divorce and finding a new job. It would be simple to move on if we could simply remove the negative element from our life as soon as we notice it. Certainly, if we find ourselves in a situation where this is conceivable, such as a new acquaintance who begins to launch the gaslighting process, we should "unfriend" that individual. However, you cannot just "block" all of the people in your life who may be involved in gaslighting behaviour. As a result, developing a strategy to deal with gaslighting in your life becomes critical. It will be required to build a suitable technique for each sphere into which you advance.

WITHIN YOUR FAMILY

Given your emotional interest in your family, this can be one of the most difficult situations to prevent gaslighting. We want to believe the best of our family, and because we love them, it's tough to believe they'd do anything as hurtful and unpleasant as gaslighting us. Many gaslighters use our family and our home as a playground, despite the fact that the home is one of the places where we should feel protected and valued. Because we have lived with our family since birth, the people in our family have had the most influence on our personality and sense of self. This also means that we are extremely vulnerable to being duped by our immediate family members. Because you already believe them implicitly, they have already traversed the idealisation phase of the narcissistic web.

Most experts think that gaslighting in the family usually involves a parent influencing a youngster in order to assert their control. If the youngster is old enough to comprehend what is going on (and hopefully has a support system to help guide and encourage them), they may take the following steps to stop the gaslighting:

DON'T FIGHT

A gaslighting parent will not be interested in your side of the storey, so don't dispute because it will only reinforce their belief that you are disrespectful–they will probably tell you this as well, with an exaggerated recreation of your comments. Declare the facts clearly and softly. If your manipulative mother has told you that you are unappreciative of her assistance and continuously moan about everything, use facts to gently contradict this. Don't get too wordy, since gaslighters, like lawyers, will find something to spit back at you in your words. Instead, explain that you appreciate everything she does and that you would try not to complain.

DON'T TAKE THE BAIT

Gaslighting is akin to baiting a bear. It's all about eliciting drama and reactions. So, if your gaslighting father tells you that you are a failure because you did not make the football team, don't be outraged. Recognize that his remark reflects on him, not on you. He is attempting to persuade you that you must be disappointed with yourself. Instead, consider what makes you happy and where your principles lay. You have successfully avoided the bait if playing football is not your primary ambition in life. It will be especially frustrating for dear Dad if you can shrug your shoulders and walk away, saying, "There's always next year, Dad." Sarkis (2019) claims that if you react in any way other than boredom and disinterest, you will be feeding their demands and enabling them to continue gaslighting.

SEEK OUTSIDE ASSISTANCE

Narcissists isolate their victims in order to manipulate the information they get and exert control over how their victim reacts. Rather than reacting to what your parents say to you, go out and confirm their facts with a credible outside source. When your Machiavellian mother informs you that you will not have a boyfriend because you are not attractive enough because you were not chosen as Prom Queen, get confirmation from another source. Don't trust her and react in the way she desires by being depressed and feeling rejected. Rather than acting, go ask a few other people what they think of your appearance.

In rare cases, we may come across a family with a youngster who gaslights their parents. Given the changing dynamics of the family context, we may see this more frequently with adult children living with their elderly parents. It is best to employ the same disarming methods that you would use at work and in relationships in these situations.

AT THE WORKPLACE

In the workplace, our emotional attachment to our coworkers decreases while our desire for validation and support increases. We all want to feel productive at work, and this is one of the areas where we are particularly vulnerable. To avoid having your ambitions destroyed at work, Hartwell-Walker (2018) offers the following disarming tactics:

BE WARY

You will be less likely to be dragged into the gaslighting scheme if you are aware of what is going on around you and gather as much information as possible. When you are in communication with all of the other office employees, you will rapidly see the truth of what a gaslighter says or does.

DON'T TAKE IT PERSONALLY—NOT IT'S PERSONAL.

It's not about you. When a gaslighter at work tells you that so-and-so is unhappy with how you dress, remind yourself that this is a falsehood manufactured by the gaslighter to make you feel inadequate. Consider whether you like the way you dress. If you do, it doesn't matter what the gaslighter is saying. Don't become furious at the insinuated slight, and don't drag the other person into it–the gaslighter is waiting for you to do so and create more drama.

SAVE THE EVIDENCE

In severe situations of gaslighting, the narcissist's rumours, gossip, and other undermining conduct can and do have far-reaching implications. It could result in a disciplinary hearing, dismissal from your employment, or even a court appearance. Prepare ahead of time. Keep documentation of everything (Sarkis, 2018) related to the drama that they have sparked against you. This will also assist you in keeping events and reality separate in your thoughts. If a coworker accuses you of making a severe error on a report, you can immediately disprove their claims by keeping a copy of the report that you can then examine. Take their word for it, but don't believe everything they say. (They may have even changed the initial report.)

AVOID SPENDING TIME ALONE WITH THEM.

When people gossip or tell stories, they usually do so when they can whisper in your ear and no one else can hear. The same is true for gaslighting. When the narcissist can corner you alone, they will most likely begin their most powerful attacks. With no one else to corroborate the gaslighter's claims, they can easily entice you into their schemes. However, if you can have someone else present when dealing with the abusive coworker, you can confirm what happened and whether or not the gaslighter was true. When the gaslighter notices that there are witnesses around, he or she is likely to avoid you.

IN A PARTNERSHIP

When we leave our family homes to build our own families or join into romantic relationships, we are subjected to even more severe forms of gaslighting from our partners. They have the ability to completely dominate and even destroy us if we are not cautious. Disarming your gaslighting boyfriend, narcissistic girlfriend, or same-sex relationship may necessitate more complex methods than those listed above.

Because of the greater proximity to the abuser in a relationship, gaslighting can be much more intense. You are much more present with them, and they may have intimate access to your feelings and memories (your past). To make matters worse, you have an emotional attachment to the gaslighter. Even if you see that something is wrong with the relationship, you still want to work on it and "fix" the problem. Disarming a gaslighter who is also your romantic partner may be far more difficult and traumatic than coping with a narcissistic boss.

The following tactics could be beneficial:

LOCATE THE PATTERN

Because you see your partner on a regular basis, you may be able to detect certain patterns of abuse. Remember that gaslighting is frequently caused by the abuser projecting their own fears and inadequacies onto you. So, if your partner runs you down when you talk about your joyful childhood and they tell you "What a terrible parent you are," you may be able to trace this back to their childhood or be prepared for future assaults in this area of your life. You'll be able to shrug off their words more easily; much like a dull infomercial, you can change the channel or mute the annoyance of their gaslighting impact. This is also likely to deter the gaslighter from victimising you more in this way.

IT'S ALL ABOUT THEM

According to Hartwell-Walker (2018), the abusers in a gaslighting environment are frequently victims themselves, and they frequently have highly painful pasts. This could be why they feel the urge to lash out and irritate others. Though this is not an explanation for their behaviour, it does explain where it comes from and may help you put their cruel remarks into context. If your lover calls you a cheat and insists that you are causing your marriage to fail, you might explore the possibility that they were the result of an unhappy marriage as a youngster. They can accuse you of something they are secretly afraid of. Their schemes are frequently about their past and their fears, rather than anything you have done.

IT'S POSSIBLE THAT NOTHING WILL CHANGE.

Gaslighters may be unable to change because of their narcissistic tendencies or because they have NPD. Certainly not without the assistance of a professional. This might be difficult to accept in a relationship since you may assume it is your responsibility to assist your partner. However, you must recognise that you are too close to the issue to do anything about it. Getting your gaslighting spouse to accept professional help may require you to support them, but it will almost likely require the supervision of a skilled expert if you wish to see any genuine improvement. Grohol (2019) discusses the usage of psychotherapy as a therapeutic option, stating that this type of treatment is primarily concerned with creating goals, developing an action plan, and developing coping mechanisms for significant psychological problems (such as narcissism). But we'll get to that later.

INSTALL A SUPPORT SYSTEM

A gaslighter's major purpose is to instil doubt and unease in their spouse. This doubt is the portal via which they can enter your inner sense of self and destroy or manipulate it. Doubt is like to an infection in a wound. It will fester over time, and you will be forced to amputate a limb or undergo surgery. Similarly, if you give your doubt(s) enough time to toy with your mind, they will infect you and cause you to lose something important (it may not be a limb, but it may be the loss of hope or confidence). According to Hartwell-Walker (2018), you need people around you who can "confirm your reality" and act as a check on the allegations thrown at you by a gaslighter to determine if they are valid before these poisoned barbs cause doubt to emerge and persist.

CONCLUSION

Being caught in the narcissistic net of trickery and deception is akin to being a fly caught in the cobwebs. Is the victim aware that when they enter the web, they will be bound up and eaten alive by something other than the fly? The correct response is "no." Moving on does not imply that you do not value your partner, boss, or parent. It suggests that you value truth and the opportunity to be more cheerful, regardless of if it involves separation. The bad thing about gaslighting is that it happens more frequently than you might think. Furthermore, it works so well that you'd be surprised to learn that scholarly and straight-thinking people fall victim—your connection with this person, which once appeared to be paradise, has now turned out to be dreadful.

There is no harmony or ecstasy in this location; only dread and secrecy remain. Your life has lost all expectations, as if the light has been out, and all you can see is murkiness and the profound dark veil of melancholy. You are currently forced to exist in a state of passive acquiescence to endure. The gaslighter's lie repeatedly subverts your perceptions of the truth, causing you to lose faith in your instincts, memory, or reasoning abilities. They are told lies, lies that reveal to them that they are overly sensitive, imagining, silly, senseless, over-responding, and have no choice but to be annoyed. Hearing this on multiple occasions brings their existence back to the forefront, and they begin to accept that this may all be true.

The narcissist's psychological abuse and repressive methods have mastered the art of instilling in their victim an exceptional sense of discomfort and disarray to the point where they no longer trust their memory, recognition, or judgement. They are a prisoner in this state. Nonetheless, many people figure out how to get the courage to break free, but this is usually after a few difficult endeavours. However, when they finally get a break, they may be able to find their way to the therapy room in time. Remaining in a toxic relationship can break our spirits, but admitting you deserve a better relationship? That is very liberating.

In general, we have the right to be in a stable relationship in which we are valued and treated affectionately. You should never have to bargain with someone who mistreats you. There's someone else out there who will treat you better. Furthermore, delayed toxic connections can have long-term negative effects on our psychological well-being, making us feel useless or insignificant.

I am always amazed by the human spirit's tenacity. I strongly urge you to take action. Seek the assistance of a specialist who can assist you in determining what is going on and the best design methods to protect yourself, preserve a record of negotiations (in writing, if possible,) or include other individuals to have ears other than yours listening in on the dialogue. Be proactive, put a stop to the crazy, and you will be able to live a happy and secure life.

CPSIA information can be obtained
at www.ICGtesting.com
Printed in the USA
LVHW062044010422
714993LV00002B/5